Real Words

Urban Poems

Written by
Jonathan Williams

PublishAmerica
Baltimore

ISBN: 1-4241-8301-4
PUBLISHED BY PUBLISHAMERICA, LLLP
www.publishamerica.com
Baltimore

Printed in the United States of America

Real Words

Urban Poems

Written by
Jonathan Williams

This is a collective verbal approach of visionary thoughts and possible experiences combined in poetic and rhyme format, using a very diverse method of the urban and conservative culture from which has never been blended together to illustrate possible unification to reach every one of all walks of life and possibly endure one vision.

1: Spot Light:

Now dreams are something that are fictional or something you want to be
Now there are dreams that can come true, those dreams for you and me
For every women, man, and child we have dreams we want or had
But what ever we all make of it, it can turn out good or bad
But for every dream there is a price you have to pay
And when you're standing on the top, everything seems to go your way
But there is a price in life, now that the top is in your sight
And when you pay for that price you think that life just isn't right
But now you paid so hold your might, don't let the price hold you uptight
Just keep the top still in your sight, and keep your mind just seeking for, just seeking for
Just seeking for that spot light

2: Our Life:

Our life is something that we have to endure
For sure, we have to think about it more
We got one life to live, so, we can't blow it
You want to live full you have to show it
You don't get older by being dumb
The knowledge is there so come and get some
Beating up on each other is out of season
We don't always agree so we try to reason
Think before you speak because everyone has feelings
Life is short when you're wheeling and dealing
You are what you eat you eat what you are
Don't ruin your entire life on trying to be a star
Don't base your life on hate base it on love
Only one rules and that is the one above
And that is the one that had put colour on earth
And everyone is a descendent from birth
So when you think about it we all have to live
Life isn't nothing to take it is something we give

3: Our Music:

In the beginning there was life and God created man
And with that life he gave him brains and inventions had began
The invention of the wheel was a contribution
But the invention of the car was a revolution
And with his eye he saw a bird in the sky
So he invented a plane so a man could fly
But music was made to calm the savage beast
And with the mind of man it will never decease
When the rhythms and the lyrics start to merge
Sometimes it sounds sweet sometimes absurd
But as years went on music had to compete
The continuation of new music made it obsolete
So call it what you want but please don't abuse it
It's not like his but it's our music

4: When the Morning Comes:

Right now relax lay down your head
Let me be your guide to this warm bed
But if this is not the place for relaxing pleasure
Let your imagination ride to limitless measure
Imagine pretend on how it would be
For me to put you in ecstasy
Your eyes will stay closed your body sexually posed
What will happen next nobody knows
Except me, I'll give your body such a thrill
You never knew something like this would feel so real
Don't take a peek because it's my surprise
You could ruin the entire moment if you open your eyes
You never want it to end even when it begins
But can you imagine. When the morning comes

5: The Crib:

Columbia ave. was my place of birth
My first foot on earth it's a lot for what it's worth
I'll never forget my first day in school man I was a fool
I broke a golden rule
Don't take a brother for a joke he'll put you in your place
I thought he was playing he punched me dead in my face
So from then on and then on I had to be tough
Because the brothers from Wilson park took no stuff
Tasker Home projects was my place to chill
With Darrell, Nate, PeeWee, Charles, Art, Ed, Will
With Gidget, Marcella, Charlette and Alberta
Oh that Yevette, I thought I had to hurt her
But one day I had to move away from where I once lived
But I will never forget the place I used to call the crib

6: The System:

The way the system is used it is so abused
One day it will blow a fuse
It is so political and so unfair
There are people who benefit and they don't care
The system will spot you, then it will watch you
The next thing you know the system has got you
It will never go away so they say
So we dream for a brighter day
But knowing all of this is nothing strange
We try to change and rearrange the system

7: The Macho Man:

Bench pressing no messing around
No less than three hundred pounds
I'll take glass chew it up very fast
Sit in a blood bath and start to laugh
It's my belief to brush my teeth
With a palm tree leaf
And gargle with ammonia
And breathe it all on you
I'll drink a dozen raw eggs in just one swallow
Every pulp in a gulp with nothing to follow
I'll wrestle with a bulldog swim with a bullfrog
Jog on a log ride a hog in the fog
So if you don't know who the heck I am
To the world and myself I'm the macho man

8: Hypnotizing Body:

She wasn't blessed with beauty she wasn't blessed with brains
The silly things she do and say just drive me insane
Most women ask and wonder they don't know what it can be
But must guys always seem to understand why you attract to me
Because your body is hypnotizing it's moving fast
Your body is hypnotizing that hourglass
Your body is hypnotizing I'm in a trance
Your body is hypnotizing it makes me dance
You are an angel in disguise
Because your body got me hypnotized

9: The Beat:

Can you hear it its loud
Pumping the crowd and I'm proud
To be part of this groove making you move
So smooth
People asking me how right here and now
How I make the girls say ow!
But it's not very easy
I need assistance from the B.E.A.T
My rhyming is always on timing
But the beat helps me keep climbing
So I have a few minutes to rock
Now give me the floor and I will make it hot
Because, there is no time to waste
I'm dancing in a fast pace
I'm going rock this place
It's so easy like 1,2,3
But I have to hear a beat

10: Prophecy:

Enter the groove of techno
Like a roller coaster up and down here we go
Oh no I took a trip unknown
I'm on the microphone so I have to be stoned
I'll take you higher than the ozone layer
Your head will spin like a record player
May I take you to the moon or Mars
Ride the milky-way and play with the stars
You're in the galaxy like a meteorite
And everything is such a hell of a sight
People will call you strange
And your visions will never change
So come tell the world and me
What is going to be our prophecy?

11: My Year:

There was a time in my life I didn't know where I was going
Or what image I should be showing
So I had to make up my mind, on what direction I should take
And what decisions I should make
Now I will let everyone know what time it is, and it is
My year, I know I have to come out my shell because it is
My year, it is the time to say what the hell because it is
My year, it is the time to have no fear, because it is
My year, the world will be surprised of what they hear, it is
My year, world come and get some because here I come
People always tried to put me down they didn't like the things I do
Saying things that weren't true
So I didn't make a sound, I took every thing they said
And placed it in my head, and I let them know what time it is, it is
My year, everybody look at me because it is
My year, behold of what your eyes can see because it is
My year, no more half stepping this time, because it is
My year, and finally I had made up my mind, it is
My year, now finally I will be the man because it is
My year, and soon you will know who I am

12: My Turn:

My time had started when it hit midnight
So I clinched my hands with all my might
Because there's nothing in the world that can stop me now
You can call all the best and they wouldn't know how
It's my turn and I will earn
Money, recognition, so stop, listen and learn
To every word, syllable, verb and noun
There's not a mistake in my words that will be found
That's how I take advantage of any beat
Speed it up, slow it down you can't defeat
Master of verbal choreography
I'm called the last dragon for the B.E.A.T
Because when I speak I don't stutter, I'm smoother than butter
When you listen to my words you want to throw yours in the gutter
Take a skill craft, a five by eight pad
Then you'll take my advise like I'm your dad
My advise to you is to squeal and squirm
Like fire you'll burn because it's my turn

13: Premiere:

Strong, weak is obsolete
Ladies and gentlemen welcome to the premiere of the year
My modal of the year is sure enough clear
Which is never too late to educate?
The mind, not with a rhyme or a sign
But to find
You'll reach your peak, but don't be weak
Be fresh with the flesh
Get you're own, together or alone
It doesn't matter all the oppositions will scatter
Some say I sound mad as a hatter
But those who say can't comprehend
What I have within
Love not hate, a spine of vertebrae
No bitterness of a rebel, most can't reach my level
An over achiever a biblical believer
Strong as an ox, muscles of rocks
The mental capacity to over whelm the greatest minds of all times
I'm telling the truth, I still have my youth
There's nothing I lack, I'm proud and black
All music I love, a gift from above
So when your hear a thundering roar
By the help of the all mighty I'm rocking once more
With protégé's all the way with equivalent status
That is why weak apparatus is always coming at us
But competition is something that no man can ignore
But music takes from the rich and gives to the poor
With more we sore the battle we won
And always remember diverse music has just begun

14: On the Run:

You're loose from a hang man's noose
Olay to O.J. but I'm the man with juice
Like Bruce I'll enter the dragon
My words get tighter while yours keep sagging
Lagging dipping you're dippy dip dripping
You're skating on thin ice and you keep slipping
Hoping and scooping for a come back
But you're scrumming on a bum track
Skeet beats with no momentum with in them
Rhythms you have to get in them and then um
You're bad vibes they just kill me
Touch the groove and ask can you feel me
Busters cluster when they hear me drop
They said I was marked but do you think I stop
Never and never and never
Because this is one groove that is too clever
People don't really try to feel me this is why I'm on the run
I heard they even tried to kill me that is why I'm on the run
I'm on the run

15: The Mood:

I took theatrics and drama in school
I guess that's why I act like a fool
I rule with a little royal crown, I start to clown immensely
With a little Hennessey
Give me some coffee and make it black
I just can't react to a show that was wack
You lack many qualities a good scholar would need
If I were suicide I would start to bleed
Indeed no need for the joy juice stream
But that it what it seems and it starts to gleam
Sometimes I need a chaser after very bad food
But I do now and then need foul substance to put me in the mood

16: The Explanation:

Let me explain my situation
I know it seems like that I'm in desperation
But that is not the case I can anxiously wait
But your love I can anticipate
Because your eyes are wondering when the moment comes
I can tell I feel the beat drums
Of your heart it's tearing you apart
The beats won't stop even when I start
Slowly with every single touch
Every move I make means to you so much
The moon gives your body a magical glow
The curves on your body looks like a light show
Now this seems like a dramatic situation
But my deep feelings for you is my explanation

17: Can You Imagine?

I said enough words to convince
We was waiting for this moment ever since
We saw each so let's not waste no time
You make me naturally yours I'll make you naturally mine
If you want to take it slow then I'll understand
But understand this girl I want to be your man
I want to have more nights to see you bump and groove
I want to have more nights to see your body
I want to see you more just naturally
I want to see you more baby of course with me
The feelings I have I just cannot hide
And every word that I mentioned came from inside
I was told it's not a sin to show what love you have with in
So when it all comes out can you imagine, can you imagine

18: Party:

Time won't wait don't hesitate
Do it before it's too late
Party that is your reason
Any time is party season
Move you need a beat with tempo
And some rhythms with gusto
And friends and family included
Because this is part of life deeply rooted
So damn time is up
Did you enjoy your life? Yup

19: Let's Live:

So to all the people that is trying to live
Adlib to the message that I am trying to give
Life is a gift in itself
Live for the health not the wealth
Do your best to go for things you really dream of
Don't forget to spread the message that we call love
It's cool to have fun and don't forget to give
So let's come alive because we have to live

20: End of the Show:

One more time here we go
This is the end of the show
But before I leave I must achieve one more task
I hope you might ask
To all the old and young lets exhort your tongues
To the song that was sung
Scream, shout yell from here to hell
We might as well
Yell out our frustrations
Through out all nations
Not shout out war but shout out peace
This might help a little to say the least
So tonight is the night we are going to do it right
Let's scream with all our might
To hate, war, greed we all yell no
This how we begin the end of the show

21: Being Down:

I'm making them up quicker and slicker
With more flavours than life savers
Timberland boots strapped brothers packing gap
Give me dap, give me dap, give me dap
We call it wack in your foot tracks to have kackies in the house
Aunt jamma would have drama with doobies all about
Receiving smoke eye from the ill
But I'm packing nine I'm doing fine but I'll chill
Indus gas full blast
But I'll pass
A paper bag brew will do
Drip a few
For the brothers in the other place
Let them get a taste ace
Known to hold them and meld them
I'll make your girl grab my groan and hold them
Like a pimp I'm serving preppies before they are prepped
But if the jimmies are not packing they can step, I'm being down

22: Success:

Success is my middle name
Give me a star on the ground for the walk of fame
Give me an autograph book with my name I'll stamp
I'll write music for you that Mozart can't
I pulled punk cards from writers long ago
Billy Joel, Prince, and Barry Manillo
I'm not scared to mention names I fear fear it self
And messing with me is not good for your health
Strive for your goals and don't settle for less
And that is the secret of success

23: Rollin':

Mother-ship rollin' three wheelin' on a ramp
And at the same time punk cards are being stamped
Soapy lyric fuming the air wave
Acting like they have souls to save
I turn off the deck pop in the cassette
And put on a jam for the real rough necks
The cube is icing the naughty is on
The snoop is nixing until the break of dawn
Now I'm in like Flinn
The hotties round brown ready to do me in
And I'm ready, yes I'm ready
The only problem that I have is to hold it steady
High strung and young on the tip of the tongue
The only episode that was swung
No time to grin even when it's done
But will I see the next morning sun

24: The Scene:

Another scene will flow I take it so
Here we go like the Wild West show
There are no cuts or breaks
Now you're cookie being baked when you make mistakes
Slamming and jamming lyrics for the doomed
I feel like Caruso on an island marooned
Brothers from the streets making it large
No time for Sarge my life I took
Some false guided fear can't hide it
Somewhere in between your soul collided
Down down to the pit of spit
Reverend Ike said sike and don't give a sh**
No shorts "G" you're ready to smoke
No time to choke what up loc
Pool putt cut the winner bussed a nut
You maxed out "G" now what

25: The Product:

Customers come into my shop of goods
Test the best damn merchandise in the hood
There's no gimmick or catch
This is one item you can't take back
Packing and smacking petty scheisse
Munching and crunching an appetizer
I'm going to give everyone what they deserve
To all my customers you're being served

26: The Dark Room:

Your boss tie is black and your collar is blue
You need a place to go when your day is through
You work eight to six for a measly buck
Your bills get fat and your pay check sucks
So you go to a place to fade your gloom
So you take a little trip down to the dark room

27: Juice:

Rollin' up to your curb slimmy
You say what nerve but you still say give me
Some of that long hard and lean
Yeah you know what I mean
Fellas act like they want to step
I pull out my nine then I'm doing fine
You see I get juice from the rough necks
I got them in check and now everyone hits the deck
I got one fool who want to get some
Rat-ta-tat-tat now he's done
Now you see I'm no joke
Now brothers give dap yo' what up loc
Pass me the bottle give me some mo'
I'm sucking up Indus I have to go
No matter how I roll I just rule
Where you're from loc? The city fool

28: The Girl Next Door:

She worked in a hard ware store
She reminded me sort of the girl next door
She wore frames of a typical dame
Right away I had to ask her name
Her name was Monique I said aw that's sweet
When is the next time we are going to meet?
She stated "Here in the store when you purchase more
You can even come back when you walk out the door"
I said "Aw that's sweet and that was real special
If I was a captain you could be my vessel"
She stated "all right that's polite
But five dollars is your items price"
So I pulled out a crispy fifty
I said "That's the smallest I have with me"
She asked "Are you shopping for your mother, father, wife or son"
I replied with "none"
I stated "I'm sporting' up my crib my two story house"
Maybe baby you can check it out
She hesitated then grabbed a paper and pen
And wrote boy I want to see you again
She wrote down her phone number address and all
The she wrote please give me a call
When I walked out the store from then I knew she was a trip
'Cause she was looking at me just licking her lips

29: Nosferatu:

Coming out at night when there's no light
And now he is ready to bite
Sleeping right through the day
He'll come out at night to play with his prey
Peeping while you are sleeping
While you're snoring he is creeping
No matter where you are he is going to get you
So look out for Nosferatu

30: Daddy' s Son:

Bad bad to have a gun
But only if you're daddy's son
But daddy is gone now you're the man
But you can barely wash your own hands
But mommy grabs you and gives you the news
You have to wear daddy's shoes
You do what you can to survive
Your daddy died at twenty-five

31: High in the Sky:

Now I don't really say too much or show how I really feel
Some people think that I am shy or think I'm not for real
I never seem to show my love my affection I seem to hide
I never seem to come straight out I keep everything inside
But when I see you every day it always get me by
Because when I see you baby I'm high in the sky

32: Halloween:

One time of year when things get crazy we call that time Halloween
This is a time when things seem hazy we call that time Halloween
This is a time when people go bizzerk we call that time Halloween
This is a time when people act like a jerk we call that time Halloween
This is a time when evil roams the earth we call that time Halloween
It's the only day when doing bad comes first we call that day Halloween
The moon is full the day gets darker it's makes you want to scream
So come along let's all get crazy and make this day Halloween

33: Look out For:

Now he'll transform right before your eyes
Don't let him catch you by surprise
He'll attack you when you'll least suspect
He'll destroy your body right through your neck
He'll bite you so fast that you can't annoy it
Some girls might truly enjoy it
No matter where you go he's going to get you
So look out for Nosferatu

34: How We Live:

If I could sing a song
I would sing fir the rich, the poor, the weak, and the strong
Because I see, yes I see
The things that is going to come upon me
And I truly know
My heart will never beat forever more
And pain is the same we know for sure
I be what I can be with love and strife
And that is how we live our life

35: Constant Rhythms:

On and On I work all day
I have no time for hustle and play
In my room no rhythms to be found
I'm waiting and waiting for that certain sound
I can not sing that well
Something please ring my bell
Then it dawned on me a rhythm that is rare
A constant rhythm is floating in the air
Constant rhythms are now flowing my way
I don't know where to go
Constant rhythms are flowing my way
Let them flow, let them flow, let them flow

36: It's Real:

What people say or people do
May not be right or not be true
Sometimes I wonder what I can believe
Achieve or just leave
So I look in the sky and just pray
I hope I meet the right girl some day
And I hope she will see and will agree
The only thing I want from thee
Is that she is real, she would always know how I feel
She will always know the deal
My love for her it's real, it's real, and it's real

37: Injin Joe:

Long ago in a country were Indians fought for land
There is a story of one forgotten man
He was stronger than the great Sitting Bull, he had the heart of Geronimo
To men he was their foe but most women loved him so
His name was Injin Joe, to him his heart was free
His name was Injin Joe, but not in this country
His name was Injin Joe, He never strived for fame
His name was Injin Joe, but every women knew his name
Joe rode on his stallion and passed through a town
But he did not know his reputation had got around
Joe stopped got off his stallion and noticed people started to stare
Women smiled, men frowned but Joe did not care
But then he saw that one girl and they met eye to eye
Joe knew this was one girl he could not just deny
But one man of envy did not like what he had saw
His jealousy and hate for Joe and the love of the girl made him grab
his gun and draw
He shot Joe in cold blood that was the end of that love tale
The girl was so upset she fell to her knees and started to yell
She yelled out Injin Joe, now he lies there dead
She yelled out Injin Joe, because his skin was red
She yelled out Injin Joe, I will never be the same
She yelled out Injin Joe, I never will forget his name

38: I'm Destined:

I have to keep it rolling before it's too late
Time is strolling and it's holding my fate
My fate is destined and it's right in my face
But knowing this I still always catch a case

39: My Book:

Open up the pages and you will see
Every word you read is about me
I don't know if it will end happy or sad
What you read is true and it's not all good but not all bad

40: The Book of Issues:

Read it and weep you don't want to fall asleep
It'll give you the creeps, this tale is deep
Peep out the mind of a mad man that is getting madder
Badder, sadder without the chitter chatter
Splatter any images that cross his path
For a day and a half he'll laugh at the after math
His shoulder has a chip at any moment he'll slip
I don't think he ever had a grip
Boiling down to a dude with a bad attitude
Crude, rude, in a daily bad mood
Everyday is a page of a book to be writing
Instead of writing, I'm spitting'
About a man and his soul, totally out of control
From the day he was born his life was scorned
Never mourn the other people he affects
Neglects, rejects with no respect
What cause a man to walk the earth with a storm?
Day by day acting like it's the norm
A man with some issues that needs a look
So many of them to write a book

41: False Leadership:

Lead us now to the promise land
But you're leading our children with guns in their hands
Their protecting other lands and patrolling foreign streets
When back home people are homeless with no food to eat
Instead of having guns show our children how it should be done
Let's make peace with everyone

42: Return to the Dark Room:

I'm on the edge now barely holding a grip
A few times late received a pink slip
I didn't have the job long maybe a half year
My boss got upset when he smelled the beer
On my breath, what's left but my last pay check
Now I spend it wisely what the heck
Rent due, bills to pay but I still consume
A few shots to the dome return to the dark room

43: Make It Slurpy:

How do you want to do it?
But you have to get your body into it
Or do I have to do some work
Make my neck jerk or my hands just lurk
From the top of your head down to your toes
Anything goes when my tongue just flows
Heading down south if you want it
Put it in my face please flaunt it
Dog gone it I've done it again
I made it slurpy to the drippy dippy end

44: The Gangsta:

Plot thickens as the time keeps ticking
No time for nose picking he's into cheap tricking
Leaving bad seeds all across the state
Is it a boy or girl next one can't wait
Home girl's boo is looking for you
Left a seed in home girl not one but two
Now you're on a man's hit list
He want you in his hand's whether hit or miss
And you're just a scout for the sling man
But you take some change any chance you can
And you gone entrepreneur
On the same turf your sling man insures
Now for sure you're stepping on some toes
As long as you have ends just anything goes
Had beef with some "G"'s please when is it going to stop
Not until you hear POPP!! (Gun shot)

45: The Tab:

You're money ran out, your friends start to fade
You ask the bar owner can I have some aide
He said "I heard you lost you're job now your tab is gone
Now it's almost the break of dawn
Take my advise get your life together
Your tab with me can't last forever
My bar is forever but you're life won't be
Think about it for a minute or three"
Now you're sitting there thinking with you're eyes in a daze
You're friends are leaving while the music plays
You're asked are you doing fine
You say "You bet but I meet you at the unemployment line at nine"

46: Does Crime Pay:

Now I'm on thin ice so I have to chill
Can't sling a thing but still keeping it real
Not a ounce to bounce zig zags are packing
But the paper must keep stacking
Tracking every step I creep
Five O' on the go even when I sleep
So my peeps get me a gig at the mall
Sporting slacks in black suit jacket and all
Peeps got pull, now I'm running things
No time for jacking no time to sling
Met a shorty and she is keeping me straight
Now food on the plate isn't that great
But I'm hanging with the homie's and I'm heading out
My shorty is illing knowing what they are about
We're getting flowed hanging at the local
A certain crew got vocal
Caught at the scene but the scene wasn't funny
Case three doing ten to twenty

47: Last Man Standing:

Who am I to come out and be so bold?
From a story untold come forth and behold
And witness a true dismiss
And put everyone on a hit list
This is now a village at siege
Calling out everyone with a little prestige
You got the power you have the doe
I'm watching you closely where are I you don't know
Broad cast your ass like a poster child
Pose and expose sit back and smile
Sinister grin what is really with in?
A face of an angel that is full of sin
When I see you I start to puke
Because everything that you accomplished was a fluke
Sex thrills no skills is in demanding
When they're all finish I'm still left standing

48: Smack Daddy:

Round brown sitting in my face
A tough turd cutter smother than butter
It doesn't matter if it's brown, yellow, or white
I'm slapping that thing all night
Slapping it down until it is hard like wood
Rubbing it rubbing it until it feels good
Pain with pleasure is what I practice
Some like it soft some like it rough like cactus
Crawl up the wall like a roach on a ceiling
Now there is something large that is so appealing
Smack daddy is here and this is what he do
For all freaks this is what he does for you

49: Booty Pie:

You got me I can't deny it
If I had to buy it I might just try it
All you have to do is stroll in front of my grill
I'm under your control you have the key to my will
But still I have to be a "G"
If you cut up you come across my knee
I'll spank that rump just right
Then I'll make love to you all night
Your tears won't last it will turn to joy
The anger of a man makes a playful boy
So I have a name for you I'm going to try
How about booty pie
When did this happen to a "G" like me
Where there other booty pies there were plenty
But your booty pie has a special gift
At any given moment it gives me an up lift
Natural high to the fullest pull it
Never shooting blanks always shooting silver bullets
My loving you seem to adore
No matter how I treat you, you seem to come back for more
Or you play your little silly games
Trying to make a "G" jealous is not the same
I'll play you like monopoly your go I'll pass by
You know damn well you're my booty pie

50: Messing with the Future:

Sir do you have babies whether young or grown
If you do, do you only protect your own
If you do I have much respect
But in your position you have much more to protect
You have started something that will cause much harm
For the future of the world we must ring the alarm
Arm your babies and your loved ones it is about to go off
It's not about who is strong and who is soft
So boss so boss they say that is who you are
But a world wide bully is what you're being so far
You go to a man's house and tell him how it should be run
And when problems occur you solve it with a gun
Think about the innocent little boys and girls
Sir please think about the damage that will be done to the entire world

51: Thrill Seeker:

Now I can be a victim of circumstance
Being single and I mingle I'm taking a chance
Of meeting someone that will take advantage of me
When you're not aggressive you're a target to be
And there are some who just want to have their fun
And this is bad when you're looking for that special someone
That person that you want to be real
They want you for you and not your sex appeal
Or want you for your funds or even something deeper
I don't want no thrill seeker

52: Travelin' Man:

I'm sitting on the edge of the bed while you're laying
Your head deep asleep with a smile I start praying
I pray to God you live well but I have to go
Where am I heading right now well I don't know
I'm sitting butt naked I grab my gear and jet
Leaving nothing behind but you I won't forget
I know when you wake up you won't understand
But baby that's the life of a travelling man

53: Love You True:

I've been a fool to let you go because you were the frame of my life
Why I acted like a fool I'll never know because I pictured you as my wife
You gave eternal love from which no one can give
I'll never forget the things you've done as long as I live
You brought me up never turned me down you stood by me all the way
Yes happily you stood by me that am why I have to say
Baby I left you now I feel so blue
I came back to tell you I love you true
Baby there is no way I can leave you again
Now we'll be together until the very end
We've been together for many years until that night I walked away
We've been through laughter and many tears why I've done so I can not say
Times may be hard right now but we'll make it by
And I know we can do it and I'll tell you the reason why
You thought it through and understood that is why we're standing here today
Yes happily you'll stay with me and now I proudly say
Baby I left you now I feel so blue
I came back to tell you I love you true
Baby there is no way I can leave you again
Now we'll be together until the very end

54: Philly Streets:

Germantown, West Oak Lane was my domain
If you thought they were soft you thought insane
I thought to myself is this middle class
You go to a corner store the brothers want to kick your ass
I stated "I moved from the south side, move out my path"
The guys looked at each other and they started to laugh
So I had to prove my self with out no doubt
You get no respect unless you knock someone out
I done this a few times, now I'm not a phoney
Neither my sisters Monica, Jackie or my brothers Darrell nor Tony
Hard times, good times sometimes bitter sweet
But it is guaranteed unforgettable growing up in the Philly streets

55: The Thief:

Bills in sight money is tight
Guess what I'm going to rob tonight
Jobless and no I'm not searching
I'd rather be on the prowl just lurking
Ski mask, dark clothes soft shoes in black
What ever I take they are not getting back
Now what I'm saying it takes a thief
"Thou shall not steal" is not my belief
Midnight strikes and I'm out
Upstate is my target route
Making sure my gear is complete
I travel light but still carry a heat
I'm in and no one is home
So I roam taking credit cards and stones
This house is nice, I'm snatching I'm out
But there is one thing I had forgot about
The alarm went off when the window got cracked
Now I'm a paddy wagon sitting way in the back

56: Born to Be Bad:

Where does it start where should I begin
Of a life soon to have an end
Time bomb ticking zero soon to show
Mad man thoughts you need to know
They say every soul is born with the blessing from God
But the devil took hold and just took charge
Of a man who was born to always raise hell
From his momma's womb to his present jail cell
Well pops was gone never known to this day
Momma strung out so bills he had to pay
O.K. no school today put on delay
Momma OD'd now he is left a stray
Hey that's enough to make anyone tough
Take a bite out of crime he'll take a bite at Mcgruff
Stuff that would make a grown man cry
Did he cry for his mom he'll say "No why?"
Friends he had none, his friend was his gun
For him shooting sprees were fun
There wasn't a day in his life there wasn't trouble he got into
Everyday was an issue

57: The Spot:

Same faces in the place, you've seen the night before
Same couple slow dragging on the dance floor
The same guy is there that gave you beef last night
Staring you up and down ready to pick a fight
But you tell the bar tender give that guy a drink
He accepted it with no time to think
You're talking to the same girl you and the guy had fought about
The guy had too many drinks so you and the girl head out (But so is he)

58: The Music Viewer:

Many out there beware all shapes and colours
Old school new school they're all like the other
Bother, cover, smother all the music lovers
Oh no U.F.O.'s and they start to hover
On top of the billboards who is number one
Oh no so and so after one month they are done
Star studded air waves is flooded
At the end of the tunnel they're head budded
Don't need you any more new blood in town
He is making me richer while you fall way down
You start to drown oh I forgot you can't swim
Throw in the life raft not for you for him
I'm sitting back watching as this goes on
The industry is the player and you are the pawn
Now you're looking pitiful holding out your hand
Now I'm the man being left to stand

59: The Truth:

Variety of secret societies
Upholding and controlling many celebrities
These are the subject's people disregard
Because it's telling the truth it is telling it hard
Hearing silly songs about a man and his momma
Throwing me off the real true drama
Tides are turning underneath our nose
It is about time this subject is exposed
The majority is taking charge
And if you're down with their system then you'll be living large
If you struggle day by day you don't see it
And if you hear about it so be it
That is the way they want it they're keeping you blind
While they're steady progressing your staying behind
And all the time they're still commanding
After these words I'm maybe left standing

60: My World:

Everything is free no reason to jack
Don't like what you got then bring it back
No doe to flow no time for greed
The only thing you have to worry about is where is the weed?
People work for free to get things done
People want to work and do it for fun
Everyone is educated and finished college
We're number one in the world because we have the knowledge
Never any war with any other land
All the leaders get together with a "J" in their hand
No racism everyone is getting along
Every race creed and colour singing the same song
Everyone believes in God and the heavenly gates
No rent to pay and no bills to be late
I forgot I was asleep in a deep snooze
Then I woke up and I saw the news

61: Big Daddy:

Oh it feels so smooth
Moving our bodies together to the same groove
Simultaneously our body's just rocking
Knock knocking the boots click clocking
Just looking at it makes me want to climax
Oh baby I can't hold it back
Do I have to put it in the right place?
You say it doesn't matter, just quit the chitter chatter
And do it just do it
You'll jump higher than Michael between each cycle
And just take a deep breath
And devour what's left
I'm excited I'm looking at twin peaks
While my thighs are caressing against your cheeks
Some men are driving a bug but I'm driving a caddy
That is why they call me big daddy

62: The Stumbled Seed:

Now one day I met mean young man
About the age of fifteen and mean as he can
We caught each other's groove and we started to hang
Still slinging his rocks when the school bell rang
He said his mom is on crack and he hated school
He said he never knew his dad if he did he'll kill the fool
He showed me a picture of his mom and I almost ran
Because fifteen years ago I was her man

63: Mr. Carefree:

Cruising greyhound from state to state
No where to be on time no where to be late
Chilling first class and living care free
Where my hat lies is my place to be
Hustling and slinging to make ends meet
My feet is on the streets I'm never skipping a beat
Sweet I meet a nice honey who is game
She believes all my lies she believes my fake name
She took me to her crib because she likes my groove
Not knowing all I want to do is stick and move
Smooth I'm in with a devilish grin
I face an angel to commit a sin
She wants me to stay I say O.K.
Knowing I'm jetting the very next day
I hit it, it was good but I must depart
A carefree man doesn't have a heart

64: Boomerang:

Now there's a price of a "G" when you're playin' the role
There's a moment in his life he starts to lose control
When being a "G" his girl isn't taking it
Because one day his girl might call it quits
Enough is enough she can't take it no more
No matter how much the "G's" loving she does adore
He's pimping and macking and she knows it
She's hurt deep inside but doesn't show it
Life is getting hectic pressure coming down
She can't take it no more so she skips town
The girl is gone without saying goodbye
Deep inside the "G" cries, but doesn't care to ask himself why?

65: Strange Voice:

Your voice sounds very familiar and I need to know what is going on
I think your voice was calling me and I'm completely drawn
Your brought me here now tell me is there something I need to know
Your voice sounds beautiful and I love it and now I feel I can't let go
Is it real or is it fake please don't play no games
I want to get to know you so please tell me what is your name
Is it Cheryl or Sue or even Jan
Why are you cold when you touch my hand?

66: The Letter:

Protecting home is cool but think about the others
Think about all babies and the babies mothers
Think about the future and who will be in it
And not think about a fight and who is going to win it
Hold some babies in your arms and look into their eyes
Can you still push the button when you hear those cries?
I despise any man who can
Pull the plug on a baby from any land
And think about other lands that are deprived
We got the power while others can't survive
911 was a message for past mistakes
Fighting fire with fire how much will it take
Many were angry about the twin towers
But there're other ways to demonstrate our power
Do we have to send our babies to make our message clear?
Do we have to kill some babies to embed fear?
Intelligent negotiations should be addressed
Before death and destruction has fully progressed
So please sir think about the little boys and girls
I hope this letter reaches the leader of the free world

67: Dawn:

I was cruising never snoozing' on route 66
For a minute I wasn't in it my eyes played some tricks
I slipped into a hood not listed like it should
The situation was bad but yet it was all good
Sort of strange not arranged seemed out of the norm
Everyone in the hood was chilling' in a certain form
There were a few old houses, one store, one school, but no play grounds
Nothing modern seemed like an old town
But I was amazed on something I have never seen before
There was one block but then I saw no more
The town had no name there was nothing to be read
And you can tell everyone was wearing taupe on their head
The town was sort of small but I drove real slow
I ready to go but I wanted to know
So I asked her name and she told me Dawn
I asked why does everyone have a taupe on
She stated "So everyone would remember what their ancestors used to be"
They wear the taupe to represent for everyone to see
Now that is what I call keeping it real
But what was really going on I did not know the deal
I was slightly out of town when she told me to stop
She said "There is something that I she had forgot"
She got out of the car in the middle of the road
She said "There is something untold"
She said "It was lovely with the time we spent
But your trip to our town was no accident"
She took off her taupe I saw her head was scalped
She didn't tell me what was that about
She threw the taupe behind me I picked it up she and the town was gone
I won't forget that strange town and the woman named Dawn

68: In Philadelphia:

Walking down South Street later I will hit market
If I had a car I wouldn't know where to park it
Hanging in the arcade most of the day long
With my mind on nothing else and doing nothing wrong
I finally played all my money now I want to go home
But five thugs on the corner won't leave me alone
I can't take it, I just can't shake it
I'm crossing on a thin line I know I can't make it
Living in the city of brotherly love
But you can't call it that if you start to push and shove
My sister told me about her friend Stacy
She just gave birth to a brand new baby
She got kicked out of home now she is all alone
Hanging in the streets with no where to roam
She couldn't support because the way life is
Left the baby on a door step then she jumped off a bridge
I can't take it, I just can't shake it
I'm crossing on a thin line I know I can't make it
Living in the city of brotherly love
But you can't call it that if you start to push and shove

Completed: March 01, 2007
By Jonathan Williams

Printed in the United States
87159LV00004B/256/A

9 781424 183012